THE COMPLETE MEAT PROCESSING GUIDE FOR POULTRY FARMS

Humane Slaughter Techniques, Efficient Butchering, Equipment, Optimization, And Waste Management For Chicken Meat Handling And Preservation

JASPER MARK S.I

Table of Contents

CHAPTER 1 5
INTRODUCTION TO POULTRY MEAT PROCESSING 5
Overview Of Poultry Farming And Meat Production 8

Importance Of Proper Processing Techniques...................11

Regulatory Guidelines And Standards 13

The Role Of Small And Large Poultry Farms......................16

CHAPTER 2 20
PRE-SLAUGHTER MANAGEMENT...20
Poultry Handling And Transportation 22

Stress Management And Animal Welfare..........................25

Fasting And Water Withdrawal Prior To Slaughter............28

Sanitation And Biosecurity Measures 30

CHAPTER 3 33
SLAUGHTERING TECHNIQUES AND EQUIPMENT....................33
Stunning Methods: Electrical, Gas, And Mechanical 35

Humane Slaughter Practices...38

Equipment For Slaughtering: Tools And Technology.........40

Quality Control During Slaughter.......................................43

CHAPTER 4 47
EVISCERATION AND CLEANING...47
Evisceration Process: Manual Vs. Automated 49

Removal Of Internal Organs...52

Inspection Of Carcasses For Quality Assurance 55

Washing, Decontamination, And Cleaning Protocols 58

CHAPTER 5 62

POULTRY MEAT GRADING AND INSPECTION 62

Grading Criteria For Poultry Meat 65

Inspection Procedures By Regulatory Agencies 68

Common Defects And How To Avoid Them 70

Importance Of Record Keeping In Grading And Inspection 73

CHAPTER 6 77

PROCESSING AND PACKAGING 77

Cutting And Deboning Techniques 80

Packaging For Retail Vs. Bulk Sales 82

Vacuum Sealing And Preservation Methods 84

Labeling Requirements And Best Practices 87

CHAPTER 7 91

COLD STORAGE AND PRESERVATION 91

Freezing Vs. Refrigeration: When And How To Use Each .. 91

Optimal Temperature For Poultry Storage 95

Preventing Contamination And Spoilage 99

Thawing And Handling Of Frozen Poultry 103

CHAPTER 8 107

FOOD SAFETY AND HYGIENE 107

Haccp (Hazard Analysis Critical Control Points) In Poultry Processing 107

Prevention Of Cross-Contamination 112

Safe Handling Practices For Employees 116

Ensuring Compliance With Food Safety Regulations 119

CHAPTER 9 123

    BYPRODUCTS AND WASTE MANAGEMENT 123

        Utilization Of Poultry Byproducts (Feathers, Blood, Offal) 123

        Sustainable Waste Management Practices 126

        Composting And Rendering Techniques 130

        Regulatory Compliance For Waste Disposal 134

CHAPTER 10 138

    MARKETING AND DISTRIBUTION OF POULTRY PRODUCTS . 138

        Understanding Market Demands And Trends 138

        Distribution Channels For Poultry Meat 141

        Branding And Promoting Your Poultry Products 145

        Exporting Poultry: Requirements And Documentation ... 149

THE END 153

CHAPTER 1

INTRODUCTION TO POULTRY MEAT PROCESSING

Poultry meat processing is an important part of the poultry industry that turns live birds into the chicken and other poultry products we eat. This process includes several steps that make sure the meat is safe, healthy, and good to eat. Knowing how poultry meat is processed and why it's important to follow the right steps helps ensure food safety and quality. It also helps meet the rules and standards set by the government.

The process begins when live birds are brought to a processing facility. First, the birds are inspected to make sure they are healthy and fit for human consumption. They are then slaughtered in a humane way, following strict guidelines to minimize stress. After slaughter, the birds are cleaned and prepared for further processing. This involves removing feathers, organs, and other parts that aren't meant for human consumption.

Once the birds are cleaned, the meat is cooled to keep it fresh. Cooling is a crucial step because it helps prevent the growth of harmful bacteria that can spoil the meat. Afterward, the poultry meat is cut, packaged, and labeled, ready to be sold to consumers. Some meat is sold as whole chickens, while others are cut into parts like breasts, wings, or thighs. Poultry can also be processed into other products like nuggets, sausages, or deli meats.

Throughout the entire process, following strict hygiene and safety procedures is essential. Workers must wear protective clothing and maintain clean workspaces. Regular inspections ensure that the facility is operating safely and in line with food safety regulations. These measures help prevent contamination and keep the meat safe for consumers.

Both small and large poultry farms play a role in the meat processing industry. Small farms may supply local markets, while larger farms contribute to bigger grocery chains and food suppliers. Regardless of the farm's size, the goal remains the same: to provide high-quality, safe poultry products.

Understanding how poultry meat is processed and the importance of food safety helps consumers feel confident in the products they buy. Whether coming from a small local farm or a large commercial one, the process ensures the poultry meat we eat is safe, fresh, and ready for our meals.

Overview Of Poultry Farming And Meat Production

Poultry farming involves raising birds like chickens, turkeys, ducks, and geese for their meat and eggs. Poultry meat is one of the most popular protein sources worldwide, and the demand for it keeps growing as the population increases. The process of producing meat begins on poultry farms, where birds are raised in conditions that help them stay healthy and grow properly. Once the birds reach the right size, they are sent to processing plants to prepare the meat for distribution and sale.

There are different types of poultry farms, and the meat production process can vary depending on the kind of bird and the size of the farm. Large commercial farms often use modern technology to automate parts of the production process. This helps make things more efficient and allows them to meet the high demand for poultry meat. On these farms, machines can handle tasks like feeding the birds, cleaning, and monitoring their health. These systems make the process faster and help ensure a steady supply of poultry meat.

Smaller farms, on the other hand, may use more traditional methods. Farmers may feed the birds by hand and give them more space to roam. While smaller farms may not produce as much meat as larger ones, they often focus on providing high-quality products, sometimes even selling directly to local markets or consumers. Regardless of whether the farm is large or small, taking good care of the birds is crucial. Farmers must provide proper food, water, and shelter to keep the birds healthy, as well as monitor for diseases or health problems.

Good farming practices, whether on large or small farms, are important for producing safe and healthy poultry meat. Farmers need to ensure that the birds are treated well and that the conditions in which they are raised are clean and suitable. Healthy birds lead to better-quality meat, which is essential for consumer safety and satisfaction.

Importance Of Proper Processing Techniques

The process of turning live poultry into meat involves several important steps. These steps include slaughtering, removing feathers (plucking), taking out the internal organs (evisceration), cooling (chilling) the meat, and packaging it for sale. Each of these steps is essential for making sure the meat is safe to eat. Using proper techniques throughout the process helps prevent contamination, keeps the meat fresh for longer, and ensures it is safe for consumers.

For example, during slaughtering and evisceration, it's important to handle the birds carefully. If done incorrectly, harmful bacteria like Salmonella or Campylobacter can contaminate the meat. These bacteria can cause serious foodborne illnesses if people eat the contaminated meat. By following the correct procedures, the risk of contamination is reduced, keeping the meat safe and of high quality for consumers. Proper training for workers and regular inspections help ensure that these steps are carried out safely.

Another crucial part of poultry meat processing is controlling the temperature. After the birds are slaughtered, the meat needs to be cooled down quickly to stop bacteria from growing. This process, known as chilling, helps keep the meat fresh and safe to eat. If the meat is not chilled properly, bacteria can multiply, making the meat unsafe for consumers. Keeping the meat at the right temperature from the time it is processed until it is sold is key to maintaining its freshness.

Packaging is another important step in the process. Once the meat has been chilled, it needs to be packaged in a way that protects it from contamination. Proper packaging keeps the meat clean and prevents it from coming into contact with harmful bacteria. It also helps keep the meat fresh during transport and storage, so that by the time it reaches grocery stores or consumers, it is still safe to eat.

Regulatory Guidelines And Standards

The poultry meat industry follows strict rules and guidelines to ensure food safety, animal welfare, and environmental care. These rules, known as regulations, can be different depending on the country, but they all focus on making sure the meat we eat is safe, the animals are treated well, and the environment is protected. Regulations cover how birds are raised, how the meat is processed, and how the products are labeled for consumers.

In many countries, organizations like the Food and Drug Administration (FDA) or the United States Department of Agriculture (USDA) are responsible for making sure the poultry industry follows these rules. These organizations set up guidelines that farms and processing plants must follow to make sure the poultry meat is safe to eat. For example, processing plants often have to be inspected regularly to ensure they are meeting food safety standards. This helps prevent issues like contamination, which can lead to dangerous foodborne illnesses.

One key part of these regulations is the humane treatment of animals. There are specific guidelines that processing plants must follow to make sure birds are treated with care during slaughter. This reduces the animals' stress, which is not only more ethical but also results in better-quality meat. Stress can affect the birds' health and, in turn, the quality of the meat, so treating them well is very important.

Sanitation, or cleanliness, during the processing of poultry meat is another critical area covered by regulations. Workers must maintain clean environments, wear protective clothing, and follow hygiene procedures to ensure the meat is safe. Clean processing plants help prevent harmful bacteria from contaminating the meat, making it safer for consumers.

Labeling the poultry meat correctly is also regulated. Packaging must provide clear information about the product, such as where it came from, its expiration date, and how to store it properly. This helps consumers make informed decisions when buying poultry meat.

The Role Of Small And Large Poultry Farms

Both small and large poultry farms are important in the poultry meat industry. Large commercial farms often dominate the market because they can produce large amounts of poultry meat efficiently. These farms use advanced technology and automated systems to process high volumes of meat, which helps them meet the growing demand from supermarkets and restaurants. By producing large quantities of poultry quickly, they are able to keep up with the high demand for affordable chicken and other poultry products.

Small farms, on the other hand, play a different but equally important role. They usually serve local markets and consumers who are looking for something specific in their poultry, such as organic or free-range meat. These farms often focus on sustainable farming practices, ensuring animal welfare, and producing high-quality meat. Many consumers prefer to buy from small farms because they believe the meat is healthier, better for the environment, or more ethically produced. Small-scale poultry processing plants, while not as common, help support local businesses and provide jobs in their communities.

Large and small farms together create a balanced system in the poultry industry. Large farms can produce a lot of poultry at a lower cost, making chicken and other meats affordable and accessible to many people. This is especially important for supermarkets and food service providers who need a steady supply of poultry to meet customer demand. At the same time, small farms offer unique options for consumers who are willing to pay more for organic, free-range, or locally sourced meat. This variety allows consumers to choose the type of poultry product that best fits their needs and values.

By working together, both small and large farms help meet the diverse needs of the global population. Large farms make sure there is enough poultry to go around, while small farms provide specialized products for those who want something different. This balance helps keep the industry strong, giving consumers access to a wide range of poultry products, from affordable options to more specialized, high-quality meats.

CHAPTER 2

PRE-SLAUGHTER MANAGEMENT

Pre-slaughter management is an important step in poultry meat processing that takes place before the birds are slaughtered. It involves several actions aimed at making sure the birds are treated humanely, kept healthy, and not stressed. These steps are necessary because how the birds are handled before slaughter can greatly affect the quality of the meat. If the birds are stressed or handled improperly, the meat can turn out to be of lower quality.

One key part of pre-slaughter management is making sure the birds are calm. Stress can have a negative impact on the birds' bodies, which can lead to poor-quality meat. When birds are stressed, their muscles use up more energy, which can cause changes in the meat, making it less tender and less appealing. To avoid this, it is important to handle the birds gently, reducing the amount of noise and movement that might frighten them. Transporting the birds in a careful manner, using appropriate cages, and keeping them in comfortable conditions are all ways to minimize stress.

Another important aspect of pre-slaughter management is ensuring the birds' health. Sick or injured birds can introduce contaminants into the processing environment, increasing the risk of spreading disease. For this reason, it is important to check the health of the birds before they are taken to the processing plant. Any birds that are unwell should be separated from the healthy flock. This helps to ensure that only healthy birds are processed, keeping the meat safe for consumers.

Cleanliness is also essential during this stage. Dirty conditions can lead to the spread of bacteria that could contaminate the meat. Ensuring that the birds are kept in clean cages and that the transport vehicles are sanitized helps reduce the risk of contamination. Workers must also follow proper hygiene practices, such as wearing clean clothing and gloves, to prevent the spread of germs.

Poultry Handling And Transportation

Handling and transporting poultry before slaughter is a very important part of the meat production process. How the birds are treated during this time can have a big impact on their well-being and the quality of the meat they produce. Moving birds from the farm to the processing plant must be done with care to avoid causing them stress or injury, as both can lead to lower-quality meat.

The first step in handling poultry is catching the birds. This must be done gently to avoid hurting them. If the birds are handled roughly, they can get bruises or broken bones, which not only affects their health but also lowers the quality of the meat. Special equipment, such as conveyor belts or crates, is often used to make the process smoother and more efficient. This equipment is designed to move the birds without causing them harm, ensuring they arrive at the processing facility in good condition.

Transportation is another critical part of this process. Once the birds are caught, they are placed into ventilated crates or containers that allow enough air to circulate, ensuring they can breathe properly during the trip. It's important to avoid overcrowding the birds in these crates, as too many birds in one space can lead to suffocation or increased stress. Stress is bad for the birds because it affects their health and can lead to poor-quality meat. By giving the birds enough space, the risk of injury or stress is reduced.

The trucks or vehicles used for transportation also need to be designed with the birds' comfort in mind. It's important to maintain the right temperature inside the transport vehicles, as extreme heat or cold can harm the birds. If the birds get too hot, they can suffer from heat stress, while extreme cold can lead to frostbite or other health problems. Keeping the temperature comfortable during transportation helps the birds stay healthy and calm, which results in better meat quality.

Stress Management And Animal Welfare

Managing stress in poultry before slaughter is very important for both the birds' well-being and the quality of the meat they produce. When birds are stressed, their bodies release hormones like cortisol, which can negatively affect the meat by making it tougher or causing it to lose moisture. This means that reducing stress is not only good for the birds, but it also helps produce better-quality meat.

There are several things that can cause stress in poultry. Rough handling, overcrowding, loud noises, and being in unfamiliar surroundings are common sources of stress for birds. To help reduce this, it's important that the people handling the birds are trained to do so gently. When the birds are handled with care, they are less likely to get injured or stressed. Keeping the environment calm and quiet is also helpful. Loud noises or bright lights can make birds nervous, so creating a peaceful setting can lower their stress levels.

Beyond handling, it's important to consider the birds' overall welfare. Treating them humanely at every stage of the process is not just the right thing to do, but it also improves the quality of the meat. When birds are treated well, they are less stressed, healthier, and more likely to produce high-quality meat. For example, giving them enough space, handling them carefully, and keeping them in comfortable environments are all ways to ensure their welfare.

Many countries have rules and regulations to make sure poultry are treated properly during the pre-slaughter process. These regulations are put in place to ensure the birds are handled with care and respect, from the farm to the processing plant. Following these guidelines is important not only for ethical reasons but also because they help maintain the quality of the meat.

Fasting And Water Withdrawal Prior To Slaughter

Before poultry is slaughtered, the birds go through a period of fasting. This means they are not given any food for a certain amount of time, usually between 8 to 12 hours before slaughter. The purpose of fasting is to make sure their stomachs and intestines are empty. This is important because if their digestive tracts are still full, there is a higher chance of the food inside spilling out during processing, which could contaminate the meat.

While fasting helps make the slaughter and processing cleaner and safer, it is also very important to continue giving the birds access to water during this time. Birds need water to stay hydrated, and without it, they can become stressed. Stress is bad for their overall health and can also affect the quality of the meat. If birds are dehydrated, their bodies don't function as well, and this can lead to tougher or lower-quality meat.

Water should only be taken away just before the slaughter process starts. Typically, water is removed around 1 to 2 hours before slaughter. This short period without water ensures that the birds are still hydrated up until the final stage of pre-slaughter management. Keeping this balance—fasting to empty their digestive systems while still providing water—helps ensure that the birds are healthy and calm, and that the meat processing is safe and efficient.

Fasting is a delicate process because it impacts both the welfare of the birds and the quality of the meat. If birds are fasted for too long, they may become weak and stressed. On the other hand, if they are not fasted long enough, their intestines might not be empty, which can lead to contamination during the slaughter process.

Sanitation And Biosecurity Measures

Sanitation and biosecurity are very important in pre-slaughter management. These steps help prevent the spread of diseases and lower the chance of contamination, making sure the meat is safe to eat.

Biosecurity starts at the farm and continues during transportation and pre-slaughter handling. On the farm, there are strict rules to keep diseases from spreading. This means controlling who can enter the farm and ensuring that equipment and vehicles used to move birds are clean and disinfected. By keeping the farm and transport equipment clean, farmers can protect the birds' health.

When the birds arrive at the processing plant, sanitation becomes even more important. The areas where the birds are handled and processed should be kept clean to avoid contamination. The equipment used to handle the birds needs to be sanitized regularly to remove any bacteria or germs that might cause illness. Workers should also follow hygiene rules, like wearing clean uniforms, gloves, and other protective gear to reduce the risk of spreading germs.

It's also important for the facility to have a good system in place to manage waste. This includes cleaning the areas where the birds are kept before slaughter and making sure any waste, spills, or dirt are removed quickly. By doing this, the facility prevents contamination that could make the meat unsafe.

Another key part of biosecurity is making sure that people who work with the birds follow strict procedures to avoid spreading diseases. This might include requiring workers to change clothes, disinfect their hands, and wear protective gear when entering areas where birds are kept. These simple steps help keep diseases from spreading from one bird to another or from one area to another.

CHAPTER 3

SLAUGHTERING TECHNIQUES AND EQUIPMENT

Slaughtering is an important part of poultry meat processing. It involves carefully handling birds to ensure they are treated humanely, while also making sure the meat is safe to eat. This process requires the right techniques and equipment to guarantee that the birds are slaughtered in a way that is both ethical and safe for food production.

The slaughtering process starts by ensuring the birds are calm. Stressful situations can affect the quality of the meat, so it's important to handle the birds gently. Before slaughter, birds are usually stunned to make sure they are unconscious and don't feel pain. There are different methods for stunning, including electrical stunning or gas stunning, both of which are designed to ensure the birds are handled humanely.

After stunning, the next step is to slaughter the birds. This is typically done by cutting the main blood vessels in the neck, allowing the blood to drain quickly. Proper blood drainage is essential because it helps improve the quality of the meat. This step is done carefully to ensure the bird does not suffer, and the process is efficient and quick.

The equipment used in slaughtering is designed to make the process as smooth and humane as possible. For example, automatic machines are often used to stun and kill the birds quickly and safely. These machines are set to precise settings to ensure the birds are treated humanely and the meat remains safe and of high quality. Smaller farms might use manual methods, but they still follow strict guidelines to ensure humane treatment and food safety.

Once the birds are slaughtered, they are cleaned, and their feathers are removed. This is often done using machines that pluck the feathers quickly and efficiently. The birds are then eviscerated, meaning their internal organs are removed. This step must be done with care to prevent contamination.

Stunning Methods: Electrical, Gas, And Mechanical

Stunning is an important step in poultry processing that makes birds unconscious before they are slaughtered. This ensures that the birds don't feel pain and reduces their stress during the process. There are three main ways to stun birds: electrical, gas, and mechanical stunning.

Electrical Stunning is the most common method. Birds are moved through a water bath that has an electric current. When they touch the water, a mild electric shock is delivered, which quickly makes them unconscious. This method is popular because it works well for large numbers of birds. To make sure it is effective, the voltage and current need to be adjusted properly. This way, the birds are stunned without causing them harm or unnecessary stress.

Gas Stunning is another method where birds are placed in a special chamber where the air is mixed with gases, usually carbon dioxide (CO_2). As they breathe in the gas, they gradually become unconscious. This method is often considered more humane because the birds are not handled one by one, and they lose consciousness in a gentler way. Gas stunning is often used by farms and processing facilities that prioritize reducing stress for the birds as much as possible.

Mechanical Stunning uses a physical tool to make the bird unconscious by delivering a quick blow to the head. This can be done with a captive bolt or a special percussive device. While this method is not used as much as electrical or gas stunning, it may be the best option in certain situations, like when other methods are not available. Mechanical stunning requires careful precision to ensure that the birds are stunned properly without causing unnecessary injury.

Humane Slaughter Practices

Humane slaughter practices are very important in the poultry industry to ensure birds do not suffer unnecessary pain or stress during the process. These practices are required by law in many countries and are also followed for ethical reasons. Humane slaughter helps protect animal welfare while also ensuring high-quality meat.

The first step in humane slaughter is stunning, which makes the birds unconscious so they don't feel pain during the slaughter. After the birds are stunned, they are quickly and carefully slaughtered by cutting the main blood vessels in their necks. This causes the birds to bleed out while they are still unconscious, ensuring that they do not experience pain. The entire process is done as fast and efficiently as possible to keep the birds from regaining consciousness and suffering.

Many countries have strict regulations that require poultry slaughterhouses to follow humane slaughter practices. These laws are put in place to make sure that animals are treated with care and respect, even in their final moments. Regular monitoring and inspections are often carried out to make sure that the stunning and killing procedures are done properly and in line with these rules.

In addition to following the law, treating animals humanely is also important for maintaining ethical standards in the poultry industry. Humane slaughter practices help ensure that the dignity of the birds is respected, and they help reduce the stress and suffering that can negatively impact the quality of the meat. When animals are treated well, it leads to better-quality meat, as stress can affect the texture and taste of the meat.

Equipment For Slaughtering: Tools And Technology

Poultry slaughtering requires various tools and equipment to ensure the process is efficient, safe, and hygienic. These machines and tools help maintain quality while making the process faster and more manageable.

1. Stunning Equipment: Stunning equipment is used to make the birds unconscious before slaughter. There are different types of stunning equipment, such as electrified water baths, gas chambers, and mechanical stunners. The

choice of equipment depends on the size of the poultry processing facility and the preferred method for stunning the birds. Stunning is important to prevent the birds from feeling pain during the slaughter process.

2. Killing Equipment: After the birds are stunned, special cutting machines or skilled workers quickly and humanely cut the arteries in the bird's neck. This step ensures the bird dies quickly without pain. Many facilities use automated systems where birds are hung upside down on a conveyor line, and machines make a precise and quick cut. These systems are designed to work at high speeds to process large numbers of birds while maintaining accuracy and humane practices.

3. Feather Plucking Machines: Once the birds are slaughtered, their feathers need to be removed. Feather plucking machines are used to do this quickly and efficiently. These machines have rotating rubber fingers or paddles that gently strip the feathers from the bird's body. Using machines makes the process faster than removing feathers by hand and helps keep the production moving smoothly.

4. Evisceration Equipment: Evisceration is the process of removing the bird's internal organs. This must be done carefully to avoid contaminating the meat. Specialized tools or automatic machines are used for this task, which helps maintain consistency and reduces the risk of contamination. Automated evisceration equipment is especially useful in large-

scale operations to handle many birds efficiently.

5. Chilling Systems: After the birds are slaughtered and cleaned, they need to be cooled down quickly to prevent bacteria from growing. Chilling systems, like air-chilling or water-chilling, are used to lower the temperature of the meat. This step is crucial for keeping the meat fresh and safe for consumers. Air-chilling uses cool air to bring down the temperature, while water-chilling involves placing the birds in cold water to achieve the same result.

Quality Control During Slaughter

Quality control during poultry slaughter is very important to make sure the meat is safe to eat and of high quality. Different checks and steps are followed throughout the process to maintain these standards.

1. Monitoring Stunning Effectiveness: Stunning is the process of making the birds unconscious before they are slaughtered. It is important that the stunning works correctly so the birds do not feel any pain. Quality control teams regularly check the stunning equipment, such as the voltage settings, to make sure the birds are properly stunned and that the equipment is working as it should. This helps ensure that the slaughter is humane and that the birds are treated with care.

2. Inspection for Contamination: During the slaughter process, there is a risk that the meat could become contaminated with things like feathers, feces, or internal organs. This contamination could make the

meat unsafe to eat. To prevent this, inspectors carefully watch the process to make sure no contamination happens. They also check to make sure that workers are following proper hygiene and sanitation procedures, such as cleaning equipment and keeping the area free of debris. This helps ensure that the meat remains clean and safe.

3. Temperature Control: Keeping the meat at the right temperature is important to stop bacteria from growing. After the birds are slaughtered, they need to be chilled quickly to keep the meat fresh. Quality control teams monitor the chilling systems, making sure that the meat is cooled down rapidly and kept at the correct temperature throughout the entire process.

If the meat isn't chilled properly, it could spoil or become unsafe to eat.

CHAPTER 4

EVISCERATION AND CLEANING

Evisceration and cleaning are important steps in poultry meat processing. They involve removing the bird's internal organs and thoroughly cleaning the carcass to make sure the meat is safe to eat. These tasks must be done with great care to keep everything clean and ensure the quality of the meat.

Evisceration is the process of removing the internal organs, such as the heart, lungs, liver, and intestines, from the bird after it has been slaughtered. This step is essential because leaving these organs inside could cause the meat to spoil or become unsafe for consumption. If the organs are not removed properly, harmful bacteria, such as Salmonella or E. coli, could spread and contaminate the meat. To avoid this, evisceration must be done in a way that prevents any spills from the intestines or other parts.

Cleaning the carcass is just as important. After evisceration, the bird must be washed to remove any blood, feathers, or other impurities. This step helps ensure the final product is free of dirt and harmful bacteria. Depending on the processing facility, cleaning can be done by hand or with automated machines that rinse the bird with water. Some facilities use special solutions to help reduce the number of bacteria on the carcass, which further improves safety.

There are two ways that evisceration and cleaning can be done: manually or using automated systems. In manual processing, workers use tools like knives to carefully remove the organs and clean the bird. While this method requires skill and attention to detail, it is still common in smaller processing plants. In larger facilities, machines are often used to automate these steps, which speeds up the process and can improve consistency. Automated systems can be more efficient, but they still require close monitoring to make sure everything is done correctly.

Evisceration Process: Manual Vs. Automated

The evisceration process is an important step in poultry processing where the bird's internal organs, such as the heart, liver, and intestines, are removed. This needs to be done carefully to prevent any contamination from the intestines, which could release harmful bacteria into the meat and make it unsafe to eat. There are two main ways to perform evisceration: manually or using automated machines.

Manual Evisceration is usually done in smaller poultry processing operations. In this method, workers use knives and other tools to open the bird and take out the internal organs by hand. It takes skill and experience to do this properly and hygienically. Since each bird is handled individually, manual evisceration gives workers more control over the process and allows them to check each bird for any issues. However, it is a slower and more labor-intensive method, which means it may not be ideal for large operations that need to process many birds quickly.

Manual evisceration also requires close attention to hygiene to prevent contamination from human handling or improper technique.

On the other hand, Automated Evisceration is commonly used in larger poultry processing plants. In this method, machines do most of the work. These machines are programmed to make precise cuts and remove the internal organs with minimal human involvement. Automated systems are much faster and can process large numbers of birds in a short time, making them ideal for high-volume production. One of the key benefits of automation is that it reduces the risk of contamination because there is less direct contact between workers and the meat.

With fewer hands touching the carcass, the chance of spreading bacteria is lower.

While automated systems are more efficient and reduce labor costs, they do come with their own challenges. The machines need to be regularly cleaned, maintained, and adjusted to ensure they are working properly and continue to meet strict hygiene standards. If not properly maintained, there could still be a risk of contamination.

Removal Of Internal Organs

The removal of internal organs, also known as "gutting," is an essential step in processing poultry. During this stage, several important organs are taken out of the bird, including the intestines, liver, heart, and gizzard. This process must be done with great care, especially when handling the intestines, to prevent contamination. If the intestines are accidentally punctured or broken, harmful bacteria could be released and spread to the meat, making it unsafe to eat.

Liver and Gizzard: These two organs are often kept for use as edible products. Many people enjoy eating the liver and gizzard, so in many poultry processing plants, these organs are carefully removed, cleaned, and inspected. Afterward, they are packaged separately for sale. Handling the liver and gizzard properly is very important to ensure that they remain safe and of good quality for consumption. The liver, in particular, must be inspected to make sure it is healthy and free of any signs of disease or damage.

Intestines: The intestines are more delicate and need special attention when they are being removed. The main concern is that the intestines may contain harmful bacteria, and if they are not removed carefully, the contents could spill and contaminate the rest of the meat. For this reason, it is essential to remove the intestines as cleanly as possible, without puncturing them.

In many modern poultry processing plants, automated systems are used to help with this process. Machines can make very precise cuts and remove the intestines in a way that minimizes the risk of contamination. Automated systems are often more efficient and consistent than manual methods, making them a popular choice in larger processing operations.

However, even with automated systems, regular cleaning and maintenance of the equipment are necessary to keep everything hygienic and safe.

Inspection Of Carcasses For Quality Assurance

Quality assurance is a key part of the poultry evisceration process. After the internal organs are removed, each bird, or "carcass," needs to be carefully inspected to make sure it is safe to eat and free from defects, disease, or contamination. This inspection can be done by trained workers or by machines, depending on the size of the processing plant.

Visual Inspection: In many poultry plants, workers are responsible for checking the carcasses by sight. They look closely at each bird to check for any signs of disease, injury, or contamination. This might include things like discoloration, bruising, or areas where the organs weren't fully removed. For example, if a piece of liver or intestines is still attached, it needs to be taken out to prevent contamination. Inspectors also look for any signs of infection or disease in the bird, which would make the meat unsafe to eat. By visually inspecting the carcasses, workers help ensure that the poultry meets safety and quality standards.

Automated Inspection Systems: In larger plants that process a lot of birds, automated inspection systems are often used. These machines are equipped with cameras and sensors that can quickly check each carcass for problems. The systems are programmed to detect issues like contamination, damage, or leftover organ tissue. Automated inspection is much faster than manual inspection and can handle large numbers of birds in a short time. Because the machines work consistently, they help ensure that every bird is inspected to the same standard. However, the machines still need to be properly maintained and cleaned to make sure they are working accurately and staying hygienic.

Both manual and automated inspection methods play an important role in making sure that the poultry is safe and meets high-quality standards. While human inspectors can catch problems that might be missed by machines, automated systems are very efficient and can process large volumes of birds quickly. Together, these methods help ensure that the poultry we eat is safe, clean, and free from any defects.

Washing, Decontamination, And Cleaning Protocols

After the internal organs are removed and the birds are inspected, the next important step in poultry processing is washing and decontamination. This ensures that the carcasses are clean and free from harmful bacteria. Following proper cleaning protocols is crucial to maintaining hygiene and preventing foodborne illnesses.

Washing: Once the evisceration is complete, the birds need to be thoroughly washed. This step helps remove any leftover blood, feathers, or tissue that may still be on the carcass. Most processing plants use high-pressure water sprays to clean the birds, making sure that all surfaces are thoroughly washed. In some cases, the birds might also be submerged in water baths to help wash away any remaining debris. This step is essential to ensure the carcasses are as clean as possible before moving on to the next part of the process.

Decontamination: After washing, the carcasses go through a decontamination process to reduce the risk of bacteria. Many plants treat the birds with antimicrobial agents, which are chemicals that kill bacteria, or use hot water to kill any harmful germs. This step is especially important for killing bacteria like Salmonella or Campylobacter, which are common in poultry and can cause serious illness if consumed. These treatments help ensure that the meat is safe for consumption by reducing the number of bacteria on the surface of the birds.

Cleaning of Equipment: Along with washing and decontaminating the birds, it is very important to clean the equipment used in the process. This includes tools like knives and cutting boards, as well as any machines that are used during evisceration. Regular cleaning and sanitizing of the equipment prevent cross-contamination, which is when bacteria from one carcass spreads to others. Keeping the equipment clean is a vital part of maintaining a safe and hygienic processing environment.

Hygiene of Workers: The people working in the evisceration and cleaning process also need to follow strict hygiene rules. This includes wearing clean uniforms, gloves, and hairnets to prevent any contamination. Workers are also required to wash their hands regularly and sanitize them to avoid spreading bacteria to the birds. By following these hygiene protocols, workers play an important role in keeping the poultry processing environment safe and clean.

CHAPTER 5

POULTRY MEAT GRADING AND INSPECTION

Poultry meat grading and inspection are crucial steps in processing poultry to make sure the meat is high-quality and safe to eat. These steps help keep the meat consistent in quality and meet safety regulations, benefiting both consumers and businesses.

Grading: Grading is the process of classifying poultry meat based on its quality. This means assessing various factors such as the size, shape, and overall appearance of the meat. For example, graders look at how well the meat is cut, its color, and whether it has any defects or blemishes. The purpose of grading is to provide a standard measure of quality so that consumers know what they are buying, and businesses can ensure their products meet certain standards. Grading can also help determine the price of the meat based on its quality level.

Inspection: Inspection is a separate but equally important process that focuses on making sure the meat is safe to eat. During inspection, trained inspectors check the poultry for any signs of disease or contamination. They look for issues such as improper handling, signs of spoilage, or any harmful bacteria that could make the meat unsafe. This process involves examining the meat closely to ensure it meets safety standards set by regulatory agencies. Inspection helps prevent meat that could be harmful from reaching consumers and ensures that the processing facilities are following hygiene and safety regulations.

Together, grading and inspection play essential roles in the poultry processing industry. Grading helps maintain a consistent quality of meat, so customers can expect a certain level of quality when they purchase poultry. It also helps businesses by allowing them to categorize their products and price them appropriately. Inspection, on the other hand, is critical for food safety. It ensures that the meat is free from contaminants and safe for consumption, which protects public health.

Both grading and inspection help to build trust between consumers and producers by ensuring that the poultry meat is of high quality and safe to eat. They also help businesses by maintaining consistent product standards and adhering to regulatory guidelines.

Grading Criteria For Poultry Meat

Poultry meat grading is the process of evaluating and classifying meat based on specific quality factors. This helps consumers and retailers understand the quality of the poultry they are buying. Higher grades indicate better quality. Several criteria are used to determine the grade of poultry meat, including its appearance, texture, size, shape, and fat distribution.

Appearance: The color of the poultry skin and meat is a major factor in grading. High-quality poultry should have a consistent color throughout, with no bruising, discoloration, or blemishes. The skin should be smooth and intact, showing that the bird was handled properly during processing. Any visible damage or discoloration can lower the grade because it may indicate poor handling or potential spoilage.

Texture: The texture of the meat is another important grading criterion. High-grade poultry meat should be firm and not overly fatty or defective. The meat should look fresh and have a pleasant, non-slippery texture. If the meat feels slimy or has an unusual texture, it could be a sign of spoilage or poor quality, which would affect its grade.

Size and Shape: The size and shape of the bird also influence its grade. Poultry that is well-formed and free from deformities will generally receive a higher grade. Consistency in size is important for commercial buyers who need uniform portions for cooking and selling. Birds that are uniformly shaped and sized are more desirable because they ensure consistent cooking and presentation.

Fat Distribution: The way fat is distributed in poultry meat is another key factor in grading. Poultry with evenly distributed fat beneath the skin, rather than having excessive or uneven fat, will receive a higher grade. Proper fat distribution helps keep the meat moist and flavorful during cooking. Excessive or uneven fat can be undesirable as it may affect the taste and cooking quality of the meat.

Inspection Procedures By Regulatory Agencies

While grading focuses on the quality of poultry meat, inspection is all about ensuring the meat is safe to eat. Regulatory agencies, such as the United States Department of Agriculture (USDA) in the U.S. or similar organizations in other countries, are responsible for conducting these inspections. Their job is to check the meat for signs of disease, contamination, and other health risks.

Visual Inspection: Inspectors start by examining the poultry carcasses for any visible problems. They look for things like bruising, broken bones, or unusual appearances in the meat. If they find any significant issues, such as large areas of discoloration or damage, the carcasses may be rejected or sent for further processing to remove the problematic parts. This visual check helps to ensure that only healthy, properly processed meat reaches consumers.

Microbial Testing: Along with visual inspections, regulatory agencies also perform microbial testing. This involves taking samples from different batches of poultry meat to check for harmful bacteria like Salmonella or Campylobacter. These bacteria can cause serious foodborne illnesses, so testing is crucial to ensure the meat is safe to eat. The results of these tests help confirm that the meat meets strict food safety standards before it is allowed to be sold.

Sanitation Checks: Inspectors also review the cleanliness and hygiene of the processing facility itself. They check that the equipment used for processing the meat is properly cleaned and sanitized. This includes looking at things like knives, cutting boards, and other machinery. Inspectors also ensure that workers are following proper hygiene practices, such as washing their hands and wearing clean uniforms. Additionally, they assess the facility's biosecurity measures to make sure that the environment is protected from contamination.

Common Defects And How To Avoid Them

During the grading and inspection of poultry meat, inspectors often find certain common defects. Knowing what these defects are and how to prevent them is important for keeping poultry meat at high quality.

Bruising and Discoloration: Bruises can appear on poultry meat if the birds are handled roughly or if there are issues during transportation or processing. To prevent bruising, it's important to handle the birds gently and use equipment that is in good condition. Careful handling helps avoid injuries to the birds that can lead to bruises. Ensuring that the birds are treated with care throughout the entire process, from catching to processing, can help minimize bruising and discoloration.

Broken Bones: Broken bones in poultry can affect the quality of the meat. This problem often occurs due to rough handling or incorrect slaughtering techniques. To reduce the risk of broken bones, it's important to handle the birds carefully and use proper stunning and slaughtering methods. Proper training for workers and the use of equipment designed to handle poultry gently can help prevent bone fractures.

Excessive Fat: Poultry with uneven or excessive fat can result in a lower quality grade. Uneven fat distribution might be caused by poor diet or improper raising conditions. To avoid this, farmers should monitor the birds' diet and ensure they are raised in an environment that supports healthy fat distribution. Managing the birds' nutrition and providing appropriate living conditions can help maintain an even layer of fat and improve meat quality.

Contamination: Contamination can occur at various stages of the processing chain, from slaughter to packaging. This can happen if proper hygiene and sanitation are not maintained. To prevent contamination, it is crucial to follow strict sanitation and biosecurity measures. This includes keeping the processing environment clean, ensuring that equipment and surfaces are regularly disinfected, and following good hygiene practices by workers. Implementing effective cleaning protocols and maintaining high standards of cleanliness throughout the processing chain helps ensure that the meat is safe for consumption.

Importance Of Record Keeping In Grading And Inspection

Record keeping is crucial in the grading and inspection of poultry meat. Keeping accurate records ensures that the meat has been properly inspected, graded, and meets all food safety regulations. It also helps processors track the quality and safety of their products over time.

Quality Control Records: Detailed records of the grading process are essential for quality control. By keeping track of these records, processors can spot patterns in quality issues, such as recurring defects or problems in specific areas. This information is valuable for making improvements in the production process, which can enhance the overall quality of the meat. For example, if records show a pattern of bruising or uneven fat distribution, processors can adjust their handling or feeding practices to address these issues.

Inspection Reports: Inspection reports from regulatory agencies are important documents that confirm the meat has passed all necessary safety checks. These reports are often required to comply with food safety laws and serve as proof that the processor is meeting legal requirements. Having these reports on hand helps ensure that the poultry meat is safe for consumption and meets all the required standards.

Traceability: Record keeping also supports traceability, which is the ability to track the origin and movement of the poultry meat through the supply chain. Traceability is crucial for addressing any food safety issues that may arise. If a problem occurs, such as a contamination issue, having detailed records allows processors to quickly trace the affected products back to their source. This helps in identifying and resolving the issue efficiently, minimizing potential risks to consumers.

CHAPTER 6

PROCESSING AND PACKAGING

Processing and packaging are important steps in poultry meat production. They ensure that the meat is prepared, preserved, and presented properly, maintaining its quality and safety. These stages use different techniques and practices that affect the meat's appearance, shelf life, and how it is marketed.

Processing: The processing stage involves preparing the poultry meat for sale. This includes tasks such as cutting, deboning, and sometimes cooking the meat. During processing, the meat is handled carefully to keep it fresh and safe. This step is essential to make sure the meat is in the right form for consumers, whether it's whole, cut into pieces, or made into products like nuggets. Proper processing helps maintain the meat's quality and prevents issues like contamination.

Packaging: Once the meat is processed, it is packaged to protect it and extend its shelf life. Packaging involves placing the meat in containers that keep it fresh and safe from contaminants. Common packaging methods include vacuum sealing, which removes air from the packaging to prevent spoilage, and modified atmosphere packaging, which replaces the air inside the package with gases that help preserve the meat. Packaging also plays a role in marketing. It provides important information to consumers, such as the product's name, ingredients, and expiration date. Well-designed packaging can attract customers and make the product stand out in stores.

Quality and Safety: Both processing and packaging are designed to ensure that the meat remains high-quality and safe to eat. During processing, strict hygiene practices are followed to avoid contamination. In packaging, the focus is on using materials and techniques that protect the meat from spoilage and external factors. Proper packaging helps prevent issues like freezer burn and ensures that the meat stays fresh until it reaches the consumer.

Appearance and Marketability: The final appearance of the meat is also influenced by processing and packaging. High-quality processing can result in meat that looks appealing and is free of defects.

Packaging that is attractive and informative helps market the product effectively, giving consumers confidence in its quality.

Cutting And Deboning Techniques

After poultry meat is eviscerated and cleaned, the next steps are cutting and deboning. These processes are important for preparing the meat in ways that meet different market needs and consumer preferences.

Cutting: Cutting involves dividing the whole bird into smaller, more manageable pieces. Common cuts include whole breasts, thighs, drumsticks, and wings. This step is performed with specialized knives or saws, depending on the size of the operation and the type of cuts needed.

In smaller operations, workers might use manual tools to make precise cuts. In larger, industrial settings, automated cutting machines are often used to quickly produce uniform portions. Automated systems can handle large volumes of meat efficiently, making them ideal for high-output processing.

Deboning: Deboning removes bones from the meat to create boneless products, such as chicken fillets or tenders. This can be done by hand or with machines. Manual deboning is done by skilled workers using knives. This method allows for precise removal of bones and is often used for high-quality products where appearance and texture are important. On the other hand, mechanical deboning uses machines to speed up the process, making it suitable for high-volume production. These machines can quickly process large amounts of meat, though they may not offer the same level of precision as manual methods. Effective deboning techniques are important for ensuring that the meat remains intact and to reduce waste.

Packaging For Retail Vs. Bulk Sales

Packaging is a crucial part of poultry meat processing because it affects how the meat looks and how long it stays fresh. The type of packaging used depends on whether the meat is being sold directly to consumers (retail) or in larger quantities to businesses (bulk sales).

Retail Packaging: For meat sold in stores, the packaging needs to be both appealing and practical. Retail packaging usually involves placing the meat in smaller, convenient portions for consumers. Common methods include vacuum-sealing, where the meat is packed in airtight bags, or tray sealing, where the meat is put in pre-formed trays and sealed with a plastic film. Retail packaging often includes important details like branding, nutritional information, and expiration dates. The design is meant to catch the consumer's eye and provide all the necessary information, while also protecting the meat from contamination.

Bulk Packaging: When selling meat to restaurants or foodservice businesses, the packaging is different. Bulk packaging involves larger quantities and focuses more on efficiency and handling rather than consumer appeal. This can include using large bags, cardboard boxes, or big vacuum-sealed packs. While bulk packaging might not need to include detailed consumer information, it must still keep the meat fresh and safe from contamination during transportation and storage. The focus here is on durability and practicality to handle larger volumes of meat.

Vacuum Sealing And Preservation Methods

Vacuum sealing is a popular method used in poultry meat processing to keep the meat fresh and extend its shelf life. Here's how it works and other methods used for preservation.

Vacuum Sealing: This method involves removing air from the packaging to create a tight seal around the meat. By getting rid of air, vacuum sealing helps prevent freezer burn, which can damage the meat and affect its taste and texture. It also slows down the growth of bacteria, helping to keep the meat fresh for a longer time. Vacuum-sealed packages take up less space in freezers or refrigerators, making them convenient for storage. This method is effective for both short-term and long-term storage, ensuring that the meat remains in good condition until it is ready to be used.

Other Preservation Methods: Besides vacuum sealing, several other techniques are used to preserve poultry meat:

1. Modified Atmosphere Packaging (MAP): This method replaces the oxygen in the package with gases like nitrogen or carbon dioxide. These gases help slow down bacterial growth and spoilage,

keeping the meat fresh for a longer period. MAP is often used in conjunction with vacuum sealing to provide additional protection.

2. Freezing: Freezing is a common method for long-term preservation of poultry meat. By lowering the temperature, freezing prevents bacterial growth and slows down spoilage. Properly frozen meat can be stored for extended periods while maintaining its quality.

3. Marination and Curing: These methods involve adding flavors and preservatives to the meat. Marination uses liquids and spices to enhance the meat's flavor and extend its shelf life. Curing involves adding salt or other preservatives to inhibit bacterial growth and spoilage, which also enhances the meat's flavor.

Labeling Requirements And Best Practices

Labeling is a crucial part of poultry meat processing, as it provides consumers with important information and helps processors meet regulatory standards. Here's a clear breakdown of labeling requirements and best practices:

Labeling Requirements:

Labels on poultry meat must provide several key pieces of information:

1. Product Name: The label should clearly state what the product is, such as "chicken breast" or "turkey drumsticks."

2. Ingredients: If the poultry meat has been seasoned or processed, the label must list all ingredients used.

3. Nutritional Information: This includes details like the amount of calories, fat, protein, and other nutrients in the product.

4. Weight: The label should show the weight of the poultry meat, which helps consumers know how much they are buying.

5. Processor Information: The name and address of the company that processed the meat must be included. This helps with traceability and accountability.

6. Food Safety Information: Labels should also provide important safety information, such as cooking instructions and storage guidelines. This helps consumers handle and prepare the meat correctly.

Regulatory agencies often have specific labeling rules that can vary by region. It's essential for processors to stay updated on these regulations to ensure their labels comply with local laws.

Best Practices for Labeling:

1. Clarity and Accuracy: Labels should use clear, easy-to-read fonts and provide straightforward information. Avoid using jargon or complex terms that might confuse consumers.

2. Regular Checks: Labels should be reviewed regularly to ensure they meet current regulations and accurately reflect the product. If there are any changes in the product or its ingredients, the label should be updated accordingly.

3. Durability: Labels need to be designed to withstand various storage conditions, such as refrigeration or freezing. They should not become damaged, smudged, or illegible over time.

4. Compliance: Always ensure labels meet the local regulatory requirements for the region where the product will be sold. This includes understanding any specific rules for nutritional information, ingredient lists, or safety instructions.

CHAPTER 7

COLD STORAGE AND PRESERVATION

Cold storage and preservation are essential for maintaining the quality and safety of poultry meat from processing through to consumption. Proper management of temperature and storage conditions prevents spoilage and contamination, ensuring that the meat remains fresh and safe for consumers.

Freezing Vs. Refrigeration: When And How To Use Each

Freezing and refrigeration are two essential methods for preserving poultry meat, each suited to different storage needs. Understanding when and how to use each method can help maintain meat quality and ensure safety.

Refrigeration

Purpose: Refrigeration is used for short-term storage of poultry meat. It's ideal for meat that will be used within a few days. Keeping poultry at temperatures between 34°F (1°C) and 40°F (4°C) slows down bacterial growth and helps keep the meat fresh. This method is commonly used in grocery stores and home kitchens.

How to Use:

1. Storage Location: Place the poultry meat in the coldest part of the refrigerator, usually towards the back. This area maintains a more consistent temperature.

2. Packaging: Make sure the meat is well-wrapped or stored in an airtight container. This helps prevent exposure to

air, which can cause the meat to spoil, and avoids contamination from other foods.

3. Handling: Check the meat daily to ensure it remains fresh. Use it within a few days of purchase or preparation for the best quality and safety.

Freezing

Purpose: Freezing is used for long-term storage of poultry meat. By lowering the temperature to 0°F (-18°C) or below, freezing halts bacterial growth and prevents spoilage. This method is suitable for meat that will not be used immediately or for bulk storage.

How to Use:

1. Packaging: Use airtight, freezer-safe packaging to protect the meat from freezer burn and moisture loss. Good options

include vacuum-sealed bags or heavy-duty freezer wraps.

2. Labeling: Clearly label each package with the date of freezing. This helps you keep track of how long the meat has been stored. For optimal quality, use the meat within 6-12 months. Although it may still be safe to eat beyond this period if stored properly, the quality might deteriorate over time.

3. Thawing: When ready to use, thaw frozen poultry meat in the refrigerator rather than at room temperature. This method keeps the meat at a safe temperature and helps prevent bacterial growth. Plan ahead, as thawing in the refrigerator can take several hours or overnight, depending on the size of the meat.

Optimal Temperature For Poultry Storage

Maintaining the correct temperature is key to keeping poultry meat fresh and safe. Proper temperature control helps prevent spoilage and ensures that the meat stays safe to eat. Here's how to manage temperatures for refrigeration and freezing:

Refrigeration

Optimal Temperature Range: The best temperature for storing poultry meat in the refrigerator is between 34°F (1°C) and 40°F (4°C). Keeping meat within this range slows down the growth of harmful bacteria, helping to keep the meat fresh for several days.

Why It Matters:

1. Bacterial Growth: At temperatures above 40°F (4°C), bacteria can multiply rapidly, increasing the risk of foodborne illnesses. By maintaining a temperature below this threshold, you help prevent bacterial growth and keep the meat safe to consume.

2. Freshness: Proper refrigeration ensures that the meat retains its quality and taste. Meat stored above 40°F (4°C) might spoil more quickly and develop off flavors.

How to Ensure Correct Temperature:

1. Use a Thermometer: Regularly check the refrigerator's temperature with a thermometer. Place it in the middle of the

refrigerator, away from the walls, for an accurate reading.

2. Avoid Overloading: Don't overload the refrigerator. Proper airflow helps maintain an even temperature and ensures all items are kept at the right temperature.

3. Check Door Seals: Ensure the refrigerator door seals tightly. If the seals are damaged, warm air can enter, raising the internal temperature.

Freezing

Optimal Temperature: For freezing poultry meat, the target temperature is 0°F (-18°C) or lower. This temperature stops bacterial growth and keeps the meat frozen solid, maintaining its safety and quality.

Why It Matters:

1. Bacterial Growth: At or below 0°F (-18°C), bacterial activity is halted, which helps preserve the meat for long-term storage. Even though bacteria are not killed, their growth is stopped.

2. Quality Preservation: Freezing at this temperature helps retain the meat's flavor and texture, reducing freezer burn and preserving quality over time.

How to Ensure Correct Temperature:

1. Use a Freezer Thermometer: Regularly check the freezer's temperature with a thermometer. Place it in the middle of the freezer, as this provides a more accurate reading than placing it near the door.

2. Avoid Frequent Opening: Limit how often the freezer is opened to maintain a consistent temperature. Frequent opening can cause temperature fluctuations that affect meat quality.

3. Proper Packaging: Ensure that poultry is properly packaged in airtight, freezer-safe materials to prevent freezer burn and moisture loss.

Preventing Contamination And Spoilage

Preventing contamination and spoilage is crucial for keeping poultry meat safe and fresh. Here's how to handle and store poultry properly to avoid problems:

Preventing Contamination

Use Clean Containers: Store poultry meat in clean, sanitized containers or packaging. This helps to prevent cross-contamination with other foods, which can lead to foodborne illnesses.

Keep Raw and Cooked Foods Separate: Always store raw poultry away from cooked foods. This separation helps prevent the spread of bacteria from raw meat to other items. Use different utensils and cutting boards for raw poultry to avoid cross-contamination.

Clean and Sanitize Regularly: Regularly clean and sanitize your storage areas, such as refrigerators and freezers. This includes wiping down shelves and surfaces to remove any spills or residues that could harbor bacteria.

Preventing Spoilage

Avoid Overloading: Don't overload your refrigerator or freezer. If too many items are crammed in, it can block proper air circulation and make it harder to maintain the right temperature. This can lead to uneven cooling and potential spoilage.

Maintain Equipment: Make sure that your refrigerator and freezer are well-maintained and functioning correctly. Check temperatures regularly to ensure they stay within the recommended ranges (34°F to 40°F for refrigeration and 0°F or lower for freezing).

Monitor for Signs of Spoilage: Regularly check poultry meat for signs of spoilage. Look for off-odors, slimy textures, or discoloration. If you notice any of these signs, discard the meat immediately. Spoiled meat can cause foodborne illnesses and should not be consumed.

Tips for Safe Storage

1. Proper Wrapping: Wrap poultry meat tightly in plastic wrap or foil before placing it in containers or freezer bags. This helps prevent freezer burn and keeps the meat fresh longer.

2. Label and Date: Label each package with the date it was stored. This helps you keep track of how long the meat has been in storage and ensures you use it within a safe timeframe.

3. Check for Proper Seals: Ensure that all containers and packaging are properly sealed to prevent air from getting in. Air

exposure can lead to spoilage and freezer burn.

Thawing And Handling Of Frozen Poultry

When using frozen poultry meat, it's important to thaw and handle it properly to ensure it stays safe and maintains its quality. Here's how to do it correctly:

Thawing Methods

1. Refrigerator Thawing: The safest way to thaw frozen poultry is in the refrigerator. Place the poultry in its original packaging on a tray or in a shallow pan to catch any drips. Thawing in the refrigerator keeps the meat at a safe temperature (below 40°F or 4°C), preventing bacterial growth. This method takes the longest, so plan ahead and allow enough time for the meat to thaw completely.

2. Cold Water Thawing: If you need to thaw poultry more quickly, you can use cold water. First, place the poultry in a sealed plastic bag to prevent water from touching the meat. Submerge the bag in cold water, changing the water every 30 minutes to keep it cold. This method is faster than refrigerator thawing but requires more attention. Make sure to cook the poultry immediately after thawing.

3. Microwave Thawing: For the quickest thawing, use the microwave. Follow the microwave's instructions for defrosting meat. However, this method can partially cook the poultry, which can affect its texture and quality. After using the microwave, cook the poultry right away to prevent any partially cooked parts from becoming a breeding ground for bacteria.

Handling During Thawing

Avoid Room Temperature: Never thaw poultry at room temperature, such as on the kitchen counter. This can cause the meat to warm up to unsafe temperatures, leading to rapid bacterial growth and an increased risk of foodborne illness.

Cook Promptly: Once thawed, cook the poultry as soon as possible. Do not refreeze raw poultry that has been thawed unless it has been cooked first. Refreezing thawed poultry can affect its texture and quality.

Post-Thawing

Handle with Clean Hands: After thawing, handle the poultry with clean hands and use clean utensils. This helps to prevent cross-contamination with other foods.

Avoid Extended Room Temperature: Do not leave thawed poultry out at room temperature for long periods. Always keep it chilled until it's ready to be cooked.

Cook Thoroughly: Ensure that poultry is cooked to an internal temperature of 165°F (74°C). This temperature kills any harmful bacteria, making the poultry safe to eat.

☐

CHAPTER 8

FOOD SAFETY AND HYGIENE

Food safety and hygiene are fundamental aspects of poultry meat processing, ensuring that the meat is safe for consumption and free from harmful contaminants. Effective food safety practices help prevent foodborne illnesses and maintain high-quality standards throughout the processing chain.

Haccp (Hazard Analysis Critical Control Points) In Poultry Processing

HACCP (Hazard Analysis Critical Control Points) is a method used to keep food safe by managing potential hazards in poultry processing. It focuses on controlling specific points where risks can be controlled or eliminated. Here's a breakdown of how HACCP works:

Hazard Analysis

The first step in HACCP is to identify possible hazards that could affect the safety of poultry meat. Hazards can be:

1. Biological: Bacteria like Salmonella or Campylobacter.

2. Chemical: Residues from cleaning agents or pesticides.

3. Physical: Foreign objects like metal shards or glass.

By understanding these risks, you can plan how to prevent them.

Critical Control Points (CCPs)

After identifying hazards, the next step is to pinpoint Critical Control Points (CCPs). These are stages in the processing where you can control or eliminate hazards. For poultry processing, common CCPs include:

1. Cooking Temperature: Ensuring the poultry reaches a safe internal temperature to kill harmful bacteria.

2. Equipment Cleanliness: Keeping equipment and surfaces sanitized to prevent contamination.

3. Storage Conditions: Maintaining proper temperature and hygiene during storage to prevent spoilage.

Monitoring and Verification

Regularly checking CCPs is crucial to ensure they are working correctly. This involves:

1. Temperature Checks: Monitoring cooking and storage temperatures.

2. Equipment Inspections: Ensuring that machinery is clean and functioning properly.

3. Hygiene Practices: Verifying that cleanliness protocols are followed.

Keep detailed records of these monitoring activities. This helps in tracking the effectiveness of your controls and proving compliance with food safety standards.

Corrective Actions

If monitoring shows that a CCP is not within its control limits (for example, if the cooking temperature is too low), corrective actions must be taken. This may include:

1. Adjusting Processes: Changing cooking times or temperatures.

2. Discarding Contaminated Products: Removing and properly disposing of any affected poultry.

3. Recalibrating Equipment: Fixing or adjusting equipment that is not working correctly.

Documentation

Keeping detailed records of all HACCP activities is vital. This includes:

1. Hazard Analysis Findings: Documentation of identified hazards.

2. CCP Monitoring Records: Logs of temperature checks, equipment inspections, and hygiene verifications.

3. Corrective Actions Taken: Records of any adjustments or removals of products.

Prevention Of Cross-Contamination

Preventing cross-contamination is crucial in poultry meat processing to keep the meat safe and free from harmful microorganisms. Here's how to avoid cross-contamination:

Segregation

Keep raw poultry separate from ready-to-eat foods. This means:

1. During Processing: Use different areas or workstations for raw poultry and other foods.

2. During Storage: Store raw poultry in separate sections of the refrigerator or freezer.

Use dedicated equipment and utensils, such as knives and cutting boards, specifically for raw poultry. This prevents any raw poultry juices from coming into contact with other foods.

Cleaning and Sanitizing

Proper cleaning and sanitizing are essential:

1. Equipment and Surfaces: Clean and sanitize all equipment, surfaces, and utensils that come into contact with raw

poultry. This includes cutting boards, knives, and countertops.

2. Cleaning Schedule: Follow a strict cleaning schedule to prevent the buildup of contaminants. Use appropriate cleaning agents to effectively remove any residues.

Regular cleaning helps eliminate any harmful microorganisms that might be present.

Personal Hygiene

Good personal hygiene practices are crucial:

1. Hand Washing: Employees should wash their hands thoroughly and frequently, especially after handling raw poultry. Use soap and water and wash for at least 20 seconds.

2. Handwashing Facilities: Provide easy access to handwashing facilities and ensure that employees use them properly.

Employees should also avoid touching their face, hair, or other parts of their body after handling raw poultry to prevent transferring contaminants.

Proper Storage

Correct storage practices help prevent contamination:

1. Designated Areas: Store raw poultry in specific areas of the refrigerator or freezer that are separate from other foods.

2. Sealed Containers: Keep raw poultry in sealed containers to prevent leakage. This also avoids any raw poultry juices from dripping onto other foods.

Safe Handling Practices For Employees

Safe handling practices are crucial for ensuring the safety and quality of poultry meat. Employees play a key role in maintaining hygiene and preventing contamination. Here's how to ensure they follow safe handling practices:

Training

Proper training is essential for all employees:

1. Food Safety Training: Provide thorough training on food safety practices. This includes how to handle raw poultry correctly, hygiene procedures, and why following safety protocols is important.

2. Regular Updates: Update training regularly to reflect any changes in

regulations or procedures. Keeping employees informed ensures they are aware of the latest safety standards.

Protective Clothing

Employees should wear appropriate protective clothing to prevent contamination:

1. Gloves, Aprons, and Hairnets: Require employees to use gloves, aprons, and hairnets when handling poultry meat. These items help protect the meat from coming into contact with contaminants from their clothing or body.

2. Clean and Change Regularly: Ensure that protective clothing is kept clean and is changed regularly. This reduces the risk of spreading contaminants.

Health Monitoring

Monitoring employee health is crucial to prevent illness from spreading:

1. Health Checks: Regularly monitor the health of employees to make sure they are not carrying contagious diseases.

2. Illness Policy: Employees who are sick or showing symptoms of contagious diseases should not handle poultry meat. This helps prevent the spread of illness and contamination.

Equipment Use

Proper use and maintenance of equipment are also important:

1. Training on Equipment: Train employees on how to use processing equipment safely. This includes

understanding how to operate machinery correctly and recognizing when equipment is malfunctioning.

2. Maintenance: Ensure employees are familiar with routine maintenance procedures and know how to report any issues with the equipment.

Ensuring Compliance With Food Safety Regulations

Ensuring compliance with food safety regulations is crucial for maintaining high standards and ensuring poultry meat is safe to eat. Here's how to stay compliant and uphold food safety:

Understanding Regulations

To meet food safety standards, you must be familiar with the relevant regulations:

1. Know the Rules: Learn about local, national, and international food safety regulations that apply to poultry processing. This includes understanding requirements set by agencies like the USDA (United States Department of Agriculture) and FSIS (Food Safety and Inspection Service).

2. Stay Updated: Regulations can change, so it's important to stay updated on any new rules or amendments that could affect your operations.

Regular Inspections

Regular inspections help ensure that food safety practices are being followed:

1. Internal Inspections: Conduct regular checks within your facility to ensure all food safety procedures are properly

followed. This helps identify and address potential issues before they become problems.

2. Prepare for External Inspections: Be ready for inspections from regulatory agencies. Make sure all practices are in compliance and be prepared to address any issues that inspectors might find.

Record Keeping

Keeping accurate and detailed records is essential for demonstrating compliance:

1. Document Everything: Maintain records of food safety practices such as HACCP (Hazard Analysis Critical Control Points) documentation, cleaning schedules, employee training, and inspection reports.

2. Use Records for Improvement: These records not only show compliance but also

help in evaluating and improving your food safety practices over time.

Continuous Improvement

To maintain high food safety standards, continually review and improve your practices:

1. Review and Update: Regularly review food safety practices and make updates based on feedback, inspection results, and changes in regulations.

2. Implement Corrective Actions: When issues are identified, implement corrective actions promptly to resolve them and prevent future occurrences.

CHAPTER 9

BYPRODUCTS AND WASTE MANAGEMENT

Effective management of byproducts and waste is essential in poultry meat processing to minimize environmental impact, enhance sustainability, and ensure compliance with regulatory standards. Proper handling and utilization of poultry byproducts and waste not only reduce waste but also contribute to resource efficiency.

Utilization Of Poultry Byproducts (Feathers, Blood, Offal)

Poultry processing produces various byproducts, including feathers, blood, and offal. Properly utilizing these byproducts not only reduces waste but also provides valuable resources. Here's how each byproduct can be used:

Feathers

Feathers are often considered waste, but they have useful applications:

1. Feather Meal: Feathers can be processed into feather meal, which is a high-protein ingredient used in animal feed. Feather meal is a valuable protein source for livestock and pets. It helps in improving the nutrition of animal diets.

2. Biodegradable Materials: Feathers can also be used in creating biodegradable products. This includes items like eco-friendly packaging and insulation materials. The natural properties of feathers make them suitable for these applications.

Blood

Blood is another byproduct with several practical uses:

1. Blood Meal: After processing, poultry blood can be turned into blood meal, which is a high-nitrogen fertilizer used in agriculture. Blood meal enriches soil with essential nutrients, helping plants grow better and improving soil fertility.

2. Food Products: In some regions, blood is used in the production of certain food products, such as blood sausages. These products are made following local food safety regulations and cultural preferences.

Offal

Offal refers to the internal organs of the poultry, such as liver, heart, and gizzards:

1. Pet Food: Many offal parts are processed and used in pet food. These organs are nutrient-rich and provide essential vitamins and minerals for pets.

2. Culinary Uses: Offal can also be used in various culinary products. For example, liver is often used in pâtés, and gizzards can be found in some traditional dishes. These products are popular in different cuisines around the world.

3. Specialty Items: Offal is sometimes used to create specialty items like sausages. These products can be sold in markets or used in restaurants, catering to specific consumer preferences.

Sustainable Waste Management Practices

Sustainable waste management practices are essential to reduce the environmental impact of poultry processing while making the best use of resources. By following effective strategies, companies can minimize waste, improve efficiency, and ensure a healthier environment.

Waste Reduction

The first step toward sustainable waste management is reducing the amount of waste created in the poultry processing process. This can be done by:

1. Optimizing Processing Techniques: Companies should focus on improving how they process poultry to minimize trimmings and offcuts, which are leftover parts of the meat. By refining techniques, the amount of wasted material can be reduced.

2. Enhancing Efficiency: Using more efficient machinery and processes helps make sure that as much of the poultry as possible is used. This reduces the need for extra resources and lowers waste.

Waste Segregation

Separating different types of waste is an important part of sustainable management. Waste should be categorized to allow for better recycling or disposal. This includes:

1. Organic Waste vs. Non-Organic Waste: Organic waste, like leftover meat and feathers, can be processed differently from non-organic waste, such as packaging materials. Organic waste might be used for composting or turned into animal feed, while non-organic materials may be recycled or disposed of properly.

1. Hazardous vs. Non-Hazardous Materials: Some waste, like chemicals used in cleaning, may be hazardous and need special disposal methods. Keeping these materials separate from non-hazardous waste ensures they are managed correctly and safely.

Waste Tracking

Monitoring waste is key to improving sustainability efforts. Keeping detailed records of the waste produced helps companies:

1. Identify Problem Areas: By tracking how much waste is generated at each stage, companies can figure out where improvements can be made. For example, if a large amount of waste is being

produced in one part of the process, changes can be made to reduce that waste.

2. Set Goals and Monitor Progress: Regularly reviewing waste records allows companies to set sustainability goals and ensure they are on track to meet them. This helps with long-term planning and keeps the company aligned with both its own sustainability objectives and government regulations.

Composting And Rendering Techniques

Composting and rendering are two effective methods for managing organic waste from poultry processing. These processes help reduce waste and create useful products, benefiting both the environment and various industries.

Composting

Composting is a natural process that breaks down organic waste into nutrient-rich compost, which can be used to improve soil. This is especially useful in poultry processing, where feathers, offal (internal organs), and other waste can be composted to reduce waste and produce valuable material for agriculture.

How Composting Works:

To set up a composting system, follow these steps:

1. Choose a composting site: Make sure the location has good airflow and drainage.

2. Add materials: Mix poultry waste, like feathers and offal, with other organic materials such as plant residues or

manure. This helps balance the compost pile and speeds up decomposition.

3. Control moisture and air: Maintain the right moisture level by watering the compost pile if it's too dry, and allow airflow by turning the pile regularly. This helps bacteria break down the waste effectively.

4. Monitor the process: Check the temperature and moisture levels to ensure proper decomposition. A well-managed compost pile will break down waste over time, producing nutrient-rich compost that can be used to improve soil health.

Composting not only reduces the volume of waste but also transforms it into a valuable product that can improve soil fertility.

Rendering

Rendering is a process that turns poultry byproducts, such as fat and protein, into usable products. During rendering, the waste is heated to separate the fat from the protein and other materials. The fat, also called tallow, can be used in products like animal feed and biodiesel, while the protein-rich meal is often used in animal feed.

How Rendering Works:

1. Collect the byproducts: Gather poultry byproducts like fat, skin, bones, and offal.

2. Heat the byproducts: The byproducts are fed into a rendering machine, where they are cooked at controlled temperatures.

This heat separates the fat from the protein.

3. Separate the components: After cooking, the fat is separated from the protein and water. The fat can then be processed into tallow, while the protein is turned into a meal used in animal feed.

4. Process for use: The rendered fat and meal are processed further, depending on their intended use, whether for animal feed, biodiesel, or other applications.

Regulatory Compliance For Waste Disposal

Regulatory compliance is very important when dealing with waste disposal in poultry processing. It ensures that the methods used to manage and dispose of waste follow legal and environmental guidelines. Adhering to these rules helps protect the environment and avoids legal issues.

Understanding Regulations

Start by learning the rules and regulations about waste disposal in your area. These regulations may come from local, regional, or national authorities and cover things like how to separate different types of waste, how to treat the waste, and how to properly dispose of it. By understanding these regulations, you can make sure that your waste management practices are up to standard and avoid penalties.

Permits and Documentation

Many waste disposal activities require special permits. Make sure to apply for and obtain any necessary permits to handle, treat, or dispose of waste. It's also crucial to keep detailed records of your waste management activities. This includes keeping track of how much waste is produced, how it is treated (for example, through composting or rendering), and how it is eventually disposed of. Good record-keeping shows that your business is following the rules and can be helpful during inspections or audits.

Environmental Impact

Waste disposal can have a big impact on the environment, so it's important to follow best practices that minimize harm. For example, improperly handled waste can pollute the air, water, and soil, causing long-term damage to natural resources. To reduce these risks, use environmentally friendly waste treatment methods, like composting or recycling, whenever possible. By assessing the environmental impact of your waste disposal methods, you can make improvements and ensure that your business is contributing to environmental protection, not harm.

CHAPTER 10

MARKETING AND DISTRIBUTION OF POULTRY PRODUCTS

The marketing and distribution of poultry products play a vital role in the success of poultry meat businesses. Understanding market demands, utilizing effective distribution channels, and establishing strong branding and promotional strategies are essential for reaching consumers. Additionally, meeting export requirements is crucial for businesses looking to expand into international markets.

Understanding Market Demands And Trends

Understanding market demands and trends is key to successfully selling poultry products. People's preferences for poultry change based on things like culture, eating habits, and health concerns. To meet these needs, businesses must stay updated on the latest trends in the poultry industry.

Health-Conscious Consumers

More and more people are looking for healthier food options, and poultry is often a top choice because it's a good source of lean protein. Consumers are particularly interested in products that are labeled as "organic," "free-range," or "antibiotic-free." These labels suggest that the products are healthier, and many people believe they are better for both personal health and the environment. Offering these types of poultry products can help businesses attract health-conscious customers.

Convenience

Today's consumers lead busy lives, and they often look for food that is quick and easy to prepare. This has led to a growing demand for poultry products that are ready to eat or easy to cook. Items like pre-cut chicken, marinated pieces, or frozen poultry that can go straight into the oven or pan are very popular. By offering these convenient options, businesses can appeal to customers who want to save time in the kitchen without sacrificing taste or quality.

Sustainability

Another important trend in the poultry market is the increasing focus on sustainability. More consumers are becoming aware of the environmental impact of their food choices. They are looking for poultry products that come from farms using sustainable practices, such as reducing waste, using less water, and ensuring good animal welfare. In addition, environmentally friendly packaging, such as recyclable or biodegradable materials, is becoming more important to buyers. Poultry businesses that prioritize sustainability can gain a competitive edge by meeting the needs of eco-conscious consumers.

Distribution Channels For Poultry Meat

Choosing the right way to distribute poultry products is important for making them available to customers. Poultry businesses can use different channels to sell their products, depending on the size of the business and the target market.

Retail Stores

Retail stores, like grocery chains and supermarkets, are common places for people to buy poultry products. Poultry businesses can either deliver their products directly to these stores or work with wholesalers. Wholesalers buy poultry in bulk from producers and distribute it to various retailers. This method works well for larger poultry businesses that want to reach many customers in different locations.

Farmers' Markets and Direct Sales

For smaller or local poultry farms, farmers' markets offer a great opportunity to sell directly to customers. At farmers' markets, businesses can connect with customers face-to-face, build relationships, and receive direct feedback about their products. Selling directly allows small farms to stand out by offering fresh, locally raised poultry. In addition to farmers' markets, some poultry businesses use farm shops or sell their products online to local customers. These direct sales methods allow farms to keep control over the quality and freshness of their products while reaching customers who prefer to buy locally.

Foodservice Industry

Restaurants, hotels, and catering businesses are big buyers of poultry products. Selling to the foodservice industry usually means providing larger quantities of poultry and maintaining consistent quality. Businesses in the foodservice industry need regular, reliable deliveries to serve their customers. Poultry businesses that can meet these needs often build long-term partnerships with foodservice providers. Supplying to restaurants and hotels can be a profitable channel, especially for businesses that produce large amounts of poultry.

Online Platforms

As more people shop online, e-commerce is becoming a growing option for distributing poultry products. Online grocery stores and meal delivery services allow businesses to reach customers who prefer the convenience of shopping from home. Selling poultry products online also opens up opportunities for reaching people beyond local markets, expanding a business's customer base. With the rise of meal kit delivery services, poultry businesses can also partner with companies that provide ready-to-cook meals, making their products part of complete meal packages.

Branding And Promoting Your Poultry Products

Building a strong brand and promoting your poultry products are essential to standing out in a crowded market. Effective branding helps customers recognize and trust your products, leading to more sales and customer loyalty. Here are some key strategies for branding and promoting your poultry products:

Creating a Brand Identity

Your brand identity is the overall image and message you want to convey to customers. It goes beyond just having a logo. For poultry businesses, a good brand identity should reflect the values that your products represent. For example, you might focus on themes like health, sustainability, or ethical farming practices. This can be communicated through your packaging design, labels, and overall presentation of your products. Make sure your brand message is clear and consistent so that customers know what makes your products special.

Promotional Strategies

Promotion is all about getting the word out about your products and increasing their visibility. There are many ways to promote your poultry products, and the internet offers a lot of opportunities. Social media platforms like Facebook, Instagram, and Twitter can be great tools to reach a wide audience. Creating a website for your business is another effective way to provide information about your products and make them more accessible to potential buyers.

Running promotions or offering discounts can also attract customers, especially those looking for a deal. You can also create content to educate consumers about your products. For example, you can share recipes that use your poultry products or talk about the health benefits of eating poultry. This not only promotes your products but also builds a connection with your audience by providing useful and interesting information.

Storytelling and Transparency

In today's market, consumers value transparency. They want to know where their food comes from and how it was produced. Sharing the story of your poultry farm—how the chickens are raised, the farming methods you use, and the steps you take to ensure quality—can help build trust with your customers. If you have any certifications, such as organic or humane farming certifications, make sure to highlight them. This gives customers peace of mind that they are buying safe, high-quality products.

Being open and honest about your production process helps create a positive image for your brand. Consumers are more likely to choose your products if they feel confident about their quality and safety.

Exporting Poultry: Requirements And Documentation

Exporting poultry products to international markets can be a great way to grow your business, but it requires following specific rules and ensuring that all necessary documents are in order. Each country has its own requirements for importing poultry, so it's important to be aware of these regulations before starting the export process.

Understanding Export Regulations

Different countries have different rules for importing poultry products. These rules are designed to protect the health and safety of consumers. For example, countries may have specific requirements about how poultry is processed, packaged, or labeled. Exporters must make sure their products meet the health and safety standards of the country they are shipping to. This could include guidelines on food safety, quality control, and packaging practices.

Documentation Required

When exporting poultry, several important documents are needed to ensure that the shipment meets the legal requirements of the importing country:

1. Health Certificates: These certificates are issued by veterinary authorities and confirm that the poultry products are safe for consumption and meet the health standards of the importing country. This document is often required to clear the shipment at customs.

2. Export Permits: Some countries require an export permit for poultry products. This permit proves that the exporter is allowed to sell poultry in international markets. Exporters should apply for these permits before shipping their products.

3. Customs Declarations: When shipping poultry internationally, exporters need to provide customs authorities with declarations that include details about the shipment. This includes information like what the shipment contains, its value, and where it came from. This helps customs officials verify that everything complies with the import regulations of the destination country.

Meeting Quality Standards

To successfully export poultry, it is essential to meet the quality standards set by international organizations such as the World Health Organization (WHO) or the Codex Alimentarius. These organizations provide guidelines on food safety and quality to ensure that poultry products are safe for consumption around the world. Exporters must follow strict hygiene and safety practices throughout the production and packaging process to meet these standards. Maintaining high quality not only helps meet legal requirements but also builds a good reputation in international markets.

THE END

www.ingramcontent.com/pod-product-compliance
Lightning Source LLC
Chambersburg PA
CBHW052259220526
45471CB00001B/414